The C.A.R.E. Principles

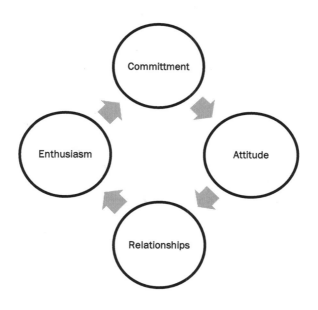

Personal and Leadership Development

John C Erdman

John C Erdman

Copyright 1984 by John C. Erdman

Revised April 1987; April 1990; April 1996; April 2010

Cover photograph by Kathy Erdman, Ideal Creative

Author photo by Julian Michael, Julian Michael Photography

ISBN-10: 0-6155018-3-4
ISBN-13: 978-0-615-50183-3
(Ideal Distributing Company)

John C Erdman

Dedication

To my loving wife Kathy who has stood by me and encouraged me to write this book. She has put up with all of my dreams and travels that made this book a reality. Without Kathy this book would never have come to light.

Praise for The C.A.R.E. Principles

This book has changed my life. Anyone who reads this book, does all the exercises and starts to practice all the concepts will experience a new awakening. The way you react to people and situations will be different. How people react to you will change dramatically.

When you become a ball of fire life has a new feel. I now wake up knowing each and every day I am filled with enthusiasm, confidence and without worry; I know that I have exactly the right tools to make my life exactly the way I want it to be. Be careful though because the new you becomes contagious and others around you will feel better about themselves. Read this book, do the work and start living life to your full potential.

Darylene Dennon, Owner, Solid Energy, Inc.
I am a Ball of Fire

John Erdman's *The C.A.R.E. Principles* is a manual for all of those things that make us happier, more productive and able to lead a fulfilling life that we were never taught in school. I've recommended it to my wife and children and would do the same to anyone that believes as John does, that you can never be enthusiastic enough. Read and use *The C.A.R.E. Principles* and prepare to be a ball of fire!

Richard Gabel, President, Humerlis Incorporated

Outstanding! I have read many personal development books and this is a definite must read. It gives you easy-to-remember concepts you can start applying to your life immediately. I have started using these principles and the results in terms of how people respond has been amazing.

Kimberley Martin, President, Stay Young 4 Life

The C.A.R.E Principles, the new revision of John Erdman's 1984 book, is a powerful blueprint for action for people who want to succeed in life. It places the reader at the controls of her or his own life, eager and ready to identify goals and move decisively toward them. John provides a model that is intuitive to understand and easy to use, one that can help anyone to succeed, using their own definition of success. The tools and real-life examples John provides in this book put it at a level above similar books; this is truly a book for **everyone** who wants to succeed.

Doug Lengel, MBA, Director of Education, Master Builders Association, Retired

We all know one or more of them: People who get up in the morning and can't wait to greet the world. We envy them, we respect who they are, their relationships and accomplishments and their ease with the world. It's often been said that the difference between a hero and a fool is the result! If you too put *The C.A.R.E. Principles* into action in your life you'll feel far more a hero and less of a fool!

How do you personally quantify success? By what yardstick do you measure your own accomplishments? Who is in control of your future? Actively following *The C.A.R.E. Principles* can help you discover all this and more*!*

The C.A.R.E. Principles is a guidebook, but just reading by itself won't get you there - you have to become an active participant! If you put John Erdman's *The C.A.R.E. Principles* to work in your everyday life, you can't help but become your very own "Ball of Fire". Your attitude and self-understanding will increase exponentially by following this program and you'll find others will be drawn to you as if by magic!

Randy Small

Pop-psych books come and go, one-off gurus of change make big splashes on the transformational stage and then dry up. They flutter around the flame of simple truth and straightforward process, and then burn out never to be heard from again. John Erdman has been teaching these rock solid, and powerful techniques for a quarter century, and now in this latest update of his book, *The C.A.R.E. Principles,* he puts an even finer edge on these time-tested transformational tools. This book is a must read for anyone truly interested in creating positive change in their life.

Alan Anderson, CHt, RH, Hypnotherapist, NLP Practitioner, transformational writer and speaker, Owner of Hypnosis Change Agent, Lynnwood Hypnosis

John C Erdman

Table of Contents

Acknowledgments

I would like to acknowledge all of the participants in my workshops over the years who have proven that *The C.A.R.E. Principles* work miracles in both their personal and business lives.

Introduction

The C.A.R.E Principles began as a talk to women's groups in the 1960's. It actually started out titled S.C.O.R.E. which stood for Self-Confidence, Commitment, Organization, Relationships and Enthusiasm. The talks soon developed into a workshop and a workbook that totaled about 160 pages. In the 70's the word S.C.O.R.E. became a negative acronym for the women's groups and the business leaders I was speaking to, so I changed the title, rewrote the workshop and workbook with the current title of *The C.A.R.E Principles*. These four principles are what all successful people use consistently whereas others only use them haphazardly.

The C.A.R.E. Principles

The C.A.R.E. Principles are **Commitment, Attitude, Relationships** and **Enthusiasm**. When we speak of *commitment* we mean having a plan and working that plan. When you reach a total commitment level you will not be swayed by the thoughts, words and deeds of other people who would may prefer not to see you reach your goals.

Having great commitment without the right *attitude* will only get you part of the way to success. Just as you are affected by the actions of other people, you are even more affected by your own thoughts and words. A positive attitude is something that requires a diligent effort on a daily basis.

Your *relationships* extend from those you love to those you might meet only once. To have good positive relationships, we must start with ourselves because "we get back what we give out in this life". Remember the great words of Jesus Christ when he gave us the Golden Rule: *"Do unto others as you would have them do unto you"*.

Enthusiasm is the spirit that draws people to us and gives us the power to get things done. With enthusiasm you can move mountains of negative thinking and negative actions away from you and bring the powerful streams of a positive life to you.

In this book you will explore all four of these principles in detail so you can begin to use them on a daily basis to become the success your potential demands. ***Your participation and involvement in this process will be the key factors which will enable you to acquire the habit pattern of success.***

Do you care enough about yourself to be successful? On the market today you will find many courses, books, CDs, on-line courses, internet searches and instructors who talk about the ingredients for success. Most businesses look for successful people and even offer some training for success. With all the materials available the question is, "Why aren't more people really successful in their lives today"?

The major reason is people have the wrong attitude about success and they are really not committed to making themselves successful. Most people today do not have their priorities in order. They work very hard on being successful in only one or two areas of their lives and forget about the other areas.

We must work on being balanced in all areas to become really successful. This is a "goal of life" and requires continual work to accomplish. Each day of our life, our positive attitude moves us toward this goal while our negative attitudes move us away from this goal.

As you move through this book you will see how *The C.A.R.E. Principles* fit into your whole life. These principles can also be taught to children to help them move along a successful path of life. When you put into use *The C.A.R.E. Principles,* you will not only influence yourself but you will influence those around you. Success becomes a contagious feeling; the more you influence others, the more they will affect your success.

You are about to embark on a rewarding experience which will clearly establish you as one of the leaders in your field. You, and you alone, will be the limiting factor. You are about to have the opportunity to make the sky (or anything else) the limit if you are willing to make the commitment!

Does Training Work?

Does having a gym membership get you into shape? Does studying a new diet cause you to lose weight? Does training work? Through my 40 plus years of accumulated experience in the training industry I have observed many training programs and participants. My conclusions are that without certain conditions being met, training or anything else doesn't give the participant a return on their investment. There may be some change or motivation in the beginning but the result doesn't last. I have discovered that there are four conditions which must be met if any training program is going to give the participant that return on their investment of lasting change:

1. **Awareness.** *A participant must know where they are in their development in order to proceed on to meet their potential. They must be able to realistically take stock of their skills and abilities in the area the training is designed to cover. They must also accept where they are in their development to be able to set improvement goals (which are necessary to get the maximum out of a training program). If you don't know where you are how can you ever get to where you want to be?*

2. **Program Content.** *The program content must be a custom designed or structured program customized (either written or verbal) to meet the needs and training goals of*

the participants. Straight off the shelf training programs rarely cover the real needs of participants. For example, how many great books have you read that didn't really cause permanent change or great talks have you heard that only temporarily motivated you?

3. **Action.** *During the delivery of any training program the participants must be taking action by participating and practicing the new material or skills. Training by osmosis does not generally work. If you don't practice, all you get is some new knowledge to place on a dusty shelf in your mind. But be careful because **practice does not make perfect - it makes permanent.** You must be practicing the right things under the watchful eyes of a good trainer or coach.*

4. **Reinforcement.** *By using active participation and role-playing the participants see themselves in light of their new skills. All training programs must have follow-up and reinforcement to convert the new skills into permanent habits. Great training programs usually produce some formal or informal mastermind groups with participants that allow the reinforcement to happen.*

By looking at any training program, workshop or seminar you are thinking of participating in, see if it answers the four conditions:

1. Does the program allow for some self-assessment of my skills and abilities?
2. Does the program or the trainers understand how to make it work for me?
3. Is the program delivered in a manner that allows for participation and interaction?
4. How does the program allow for follow up and reinforcement?

The answers will guide you in making training work for you and you will be getting a real return on your investment of money and time.

Cycle of Self-Development

Everyone moves though the cycle of self-development as they learn new techniques, both personally and professionally. You start with a need for knowledge. Then practice that new knowledge to develop the skills. Most people get stuck between knowledge and practice and don't develop the new skills. You need to practice new knowledge until it becomes a new skill, then you will start the cycle again. Just remember that *"practice makes permanent, not perfect"*.

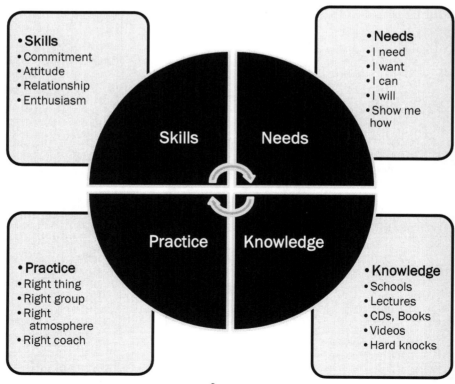

Success

As you progress through *The C.A.R.E Principles* you will find the words *success, total success* and *successful* used many times. In today's world there are many definitions for success - some of which seem to cause some people to turn off or tune out what is really being said.

The most popular definition of success is usually stated in the question, *"How much money did you make last year"?* or *"How much money will you earn this year"?* As often as this comes up there is always someone else stating, *"Money isn't everything"!*

Webster's dictionary defines success as:

1. A favorable outcome.
2. The gaining of fame, wealth, etc.

This gives you a broader scope to work with, but still seems to lack the feeling of overall goodness. It leaves out the people who feel good about themselves without a lot of money or recognition. You probably know some people who are always happy, have good home and business lives, are involved in everything, but are rarely in the limelight. Most people would consider these types of people successful, yet when asked who they determine to be successful, always name the rich and famous.

In searching for a workable definition of success I found most people liked the following definition because it deals in a positive manner with all people. It allows people to become successful by helping others become successful. *The C.A.R.E Principles* were written with this definition in mind and the philosophy by which I live.

> *Total success is the continued involvement in the pursuit of worthy goals and desires in all areas of life; realized for and through the benefit of others rather than at their expense.*

S.U.C.C.E.S.S.

Self-Image   Have a positive state of mind about yourself and your ability to achieve. View failures for their value in the learning process and then dismiss them from your mind. Unfortunately we learn, grow and expand more through the lessons taught by failure than by success. The negative aspects of failure are present only if we dwell on it. Present yourself with dignity through: *thought, word and deed.*

Understanding   Understand yourself. Accentuate your positive attributes, recognize your negative traits and change them to positive traits. Equally important is the understanding of others. See things from their point of view and you will develop the ability to transmit your ideas in terms that will motivate others. Empathy for others will help you relate in a more positive manner.

Criticize Not   Criticism solicits an immediate response of self-justification. It almost always breeds contempt, rejection and argumentativeness. In human relation concepts an argument is: *"Two fools in disagreement with one another"*. If we pay attention, we notice that life is like a mirror; what we dislike in others is usually a reflection of some aspect within ourselves that we dislike.

Challenge Yourself   Challenge yourself to grow, expand and improve. Do so personally, socially and professionally. Be tenacious in the application of diligent effort toward achievement. Challenge yourself to succeed now and forever.

Esteem   Have respect for yourself and for others. We are all individuals and must accept each other as that. We do not always have to agree with someone to respect their opinion - "as their opinion".

Sense of Direction   Goals are an absolute necessity in life. They give our life meaning, purpose and direction. We obtain a feeling of satisfaction from the accomplishment of our goals. Clearly understand the reasons why success is important, and establish action plans that move you toward your success.

Self-Confidence   Have deep faith in yourself and in your ability to achieve. Base it upon all of your past successes. Eliminate the effects of negative thoughts by reminding yourself of all of your past achievements. Do not allow the negative attitudes of others to affect you. Tell yourself: *"I can and will succeed - regardless"*.

Are You Average?

Edmund Gaudet

"Average" is what the failures claim to be when their family and friends ask them why they are not more successful.

"Average" is the top of the bottom, the best of the worst, the bottom of the top, the worst of the best. Which of these are you?

"Average" means being run-of-the-mill, mediocre, insignificant, an also-ran, a nonentity.

Being **"average"** is the lazy person's cop-out; it's lacking the guts to take a stand in life; it's living by default.

Being **"average"** is to take up space for no purpose; to take the trip through life, but never pay the fare; to return no interest for God's investment in you.

Being **"average"** is to pass one's life away with time, rather than to pass one's time away with life. It's to kill time rather than work it to death.

To be **"average"** is to be forgotten once you pass from this life. The successful are remembered for their contributions, the failures are remembered because they tried, but the "average", the silent majority is just forgotten.

To be **"average"** is to commit the greatest crime one can against one's self, humanity and one's God. The saddest epitaph is this: "Here lies Mr. or Ms. Average -- here lies the remains of what might have been -- except for their belief that they were only 'average'".

John C Erdman

Commitment

The first step in *The C.A.R.E Principles*; is becoming committed to yourself, your ideas, your desires and your goals. The word commitment strikes fear in the hearts of many people, but commitment is as simple as setting goals and action plans that have been broken down into achievable size.

Goal setting to most people is a chore they do only on a small scale, if at all. For some people, goals are something they talk about but seldom have in a concrete form. If you don't have well defined goals, you will just drift around in this adventure of life we call 'trip' Earth. **When you have well-defined goals, you know where you are going and can plan on how to get there; we define that as Commitment.** To establish the road map so you can achieve your real potential you must have written goals that ignite a burning desire.

Remember, if you do not stand for something, you will fall for anything.

Have you ever wondered why you set some goals but they never seem to come true. To explain why this happens we need to realize we function in three realms of consciousness. In psychological terms the three areas become the creative subconscious, the subconscious and the conscious. I prefer to term them the **spiritual**, the **mental** and the **physical**. An illustrated diagram would look like a target with the spiritual realm in the center, the mental realm surrounding the spiritual realm and the physical realm surrounding the mental realm.

The process starts in the spiritual realm in the form of desires. The word desire breaks down as "de" meaning "from" and "sire" meaning "father". You set a goal in the mental realm where you think about it and then set up your plans on how to achieve it. Most people stop there without moving it into the physical realm. If you do not move the goals into the physical realm, your chances of achieving the results you want are slim because you are being influenced constantly on the physical and mental realms.

To put it simply, we get our desires or thoughts from the **spiritual** or the creative subconscious. We then move them into the **mental** or the subconscious and begin to formulate them into goals. They are then put into writing so we can move them into the **physical** or conscious where we get the desired results.

The only way to move from the mental realm to the physical realm is by writing down your goals and your action plans to achieve them. You will be working on the steps necessary to bring your goals from the mental realms to the physical realms so you can begin to achieve total success.

The Major Areas in Which to Establish Goals

In order to live a balanced life your goals need to be established in all eight major areas. **The goal is to live a balanced life.** The eight major areas in which you will be working are as follows:

1. **Spiritual**
2. **Family**

3. Professional or Career
4. Physical Self-Improvement
5. Mental Self-Improvement
6. Financial
7. Social
8. Community

Steps to Establish Goals

The seven steps to establishing your goals in the physical realm are:

1. Assess the "As Is".

2. Establish the "Target Point".

3. Select the goals, set the time tables and put them in writing.

4. Commit yourself to the goals by knowing the "Whys".

5. Determine there are no conflicts.

6. Start working on the "Bite-Size" pieces.

7. Follow up and change as necessary.

Step One

The first thing we need to understand is where we are right now or the **"As Is"** situation. If you do not know where you are when you start to plan your adventure on "Trip Earth", you will draw your road map with only one road. Think for a moment of being lost; you have no idea where you are. If you have a map that shows where help is, but you do not know where you are on the map, can you use it to get out of the wilderness? Probably not.

When sitting down to write out or establish their goals, most people never bother to think about where they are in their progress. In order to move toward your goal, you need to write out where you are right now so you can establish a base line. Then we can move on to step two.

Step Two

The next step to establishing your goals in the physical realm is to decide on a **"Target Point"**. This statement will be a description of what you really want out of life. Write down what you want for yourself and your family. This statement should include all eight goal-setting areas, and be approximately 250 words in length.

Your target statement is future oriented. Describe how your life will look and feel in all eight major areas, 2 years, 5 years, 10 years or 100 years from now. The time span is up to you. Be creative and positive in your statement. Write as if someone has waved a magic wand over you and erased all your limitations. Age, sex, race or creed are no problems in this statement, in fact they can be an advantage in deciding what you do or do not want in your "Target Point" statement.

Instructions for the "As Is" Questionnaire

To help you find the "As Is" situation, answer the questions on this questionnaire. Rate your life and habits as honestly as you can about your situation right now. The ratings go from "1" to "10" with "1" meaning you don't do the item at the present time (very low commitment) and "10" meaning you do the item always (very high commitment). Circle the best answer and remember to answer as honestly as you can. You are the only one looking at this and lying to yourself will not get you to where you want to be.

The "As Is" Questionnaire

	1	2	3	4	5	6	7	8	9	10
1. Meditate or pray daily?										
2. Enjoy time with your family?										
3. Satisfied with your career?										
4. Enjoy reading?										
5. Established financial goals?										
6. Exercise daily?										
7. Established social goals?										
8. Volunteer in the community?										
9. Established spiritual goals?										
10. Write or phone family members?										
11. Work creatively at your career?										
12. Established mental goals?										
13. Earning the income you want?										
14. Established physical goals?										
15. Make friends easily?										
16. Belong to any civic clubs?										
17. Regularly attend a spiritual gathering?										
18. Established family goals?										
19. Established professional goals?										
20. Attend classes to continue learning?										

21. Have an investment plan?											
22. Eat balanced & nutritious meals?											
23. Enjoy socializing with new people?											
24. Established community goals?											

Totals from the Questionnaire

Spiritual	Family	Career	Mental
1. _____	2. _____	3. _____	4. _____
9. _____	10. _____	11. _____	12. _____
17. _____	18. _____	19. _____	20. _____
T = _____	T = _____	T = _____	T = _____

Financial	Physical	Social	Community
5. _____	6. _____	7. _____	8. _____
13. _____	14. _____	15. _____	16. _____
21. _____	22. _____	23. _____	24. _____
T = _____	T = _____	T = _____	T = _____

Wheel of Life

Now the totals from the questionnaire can be transferred to the Wheel of Life on the next page. The center of the wheel is "0" points and the outer ring is worth "30" points.

Example: If your score for spiritual was "15" you would put a dot on the spiritual line at approximately the 15 mark.

Go around the Wheel of Life and put a dot at each of the eight areas on their corresponding line. Now draw a line connecting each dot and fill in the enclosed area. Looking at the area you have drawn, the questions to ask yourself are:

1. **How balanced are you?**

2. **Are you going down the road of life smoothly or are you just bouncing around?**

3. **Now commit the results (in writing) into your "As Is" Statement and your "Target Point" Statement.**

Wheel of Life

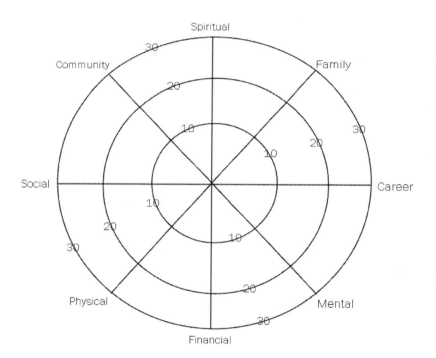

Your "As Is" Statement

_____

_____

_____

_____

_____

_____

_____

_____

_____

_____

_____

_____

_____

_____

_____

_____

Your "Target Point" Statement

_____

_____

_____

_____

_____

_____

_____

_____

_____

_____

_____

_____

_____

_____

_____

_____

_____

Step Three

Now that you know where you are and where you are going, you can select the goals that will give you the desired results. Write out what has to happen to move you toward or into the **"Target Point"** areas. Set time tables so you will know when you want to accomplish these goals, then you will not end up on that mystical island - **"Someday I'll"**. Without definite time tables, you will drift and not accomplish what you set out to do. With definite time tables, you stay on track and do the things you need to do when you are supposed to do them. Break down the goals into three areas or time increments, namely: **Long-Term**, **Mid-Term** and **Short-Term**.

- **Long-term goals** are one year long. You can control things or events one year at a time and anything longer falls into our "Target Point". The question to ask yourself is, **"What can I do during this year that will move me towards my 'Target Point'"**?

- Next, you break down the long-term into **mid-term goals**. These can be quarterly or monthly time spans and will give you four to twelve check points to gauge your progress.

- Breaking these midterm goals down even further into **short-term goals**, which are weekly or daily, and will make your progress easier and seemingly faster to accomplish. Your goals are now in **"Bite-Size"** pieces you can work with.

All of these items need to be put into writing so you have a physical record of these goals and action plans.

Step Four

Commit yourself to the goals by knowing the **"Whys"**. The only way to stay on track with goal achieving is to know why you want to achieve it. If it is someone else's goal and you did not have any part in choosing it, you do not have any real commitment in going after it. Always ask this question, **"Why is this goal important for me to accomplish"?**

Step Five

Determine you do not have conflicts in any area. When you have your goals written out you can look them over and see if they are in conflict with each other. How will achieving my goal affect others, my family, workplace and community? If you do not solve the conflicts before you start to use your goal sheets the chances of you becoming confused and disillusioned will be greatly intensified. **Now is the time to eliminate any of the conflicts.**

Step Six

Start working on the **"Bite-Size"** pieces. If you try to accomplish the long-term goal first you will become frustrated because it is too large to do in one bite. By working on the short-term goals or the bite-size areas, you accomplish things faster and it will say to your subconscious mind "I am a winner, and I do the things I say I am going to do".

Step Seven

Follow up and change when necessary. **Change and choice are the only two things that are constant in the world.** You always have change going on around you and you always have the choice on how you are going to deal with it. You can deal with change either positively or negatively. The only way you know it is time to change your goals is to follow up on a consistent basis. This means you read and look closely at your goals on a daily basis. On the bottom of each goal sheet you should print in large letters, **"It Is OK To Change"**!

Beware of the Dangers
When You Establish Goals

Your goal must:

1. Be distant and realistic for you, to avoid the frustration of failure to reach goals that have been set with too short a time table.

2. Be a personally established goal and not just "lip service" to someone else's goal(s).

3. Not be set too low for the purpose of assuring easy accomplishment.

4. Not conflict with goals you have set in other areas of your life or with your personal convictions.

5. Not have any **'Protection Plans'** built into it. Protection plans are the statements that you know are true and will happen. Such as, "I won't make sales calls if it is raining". If you live in a rainy part of the country you don't have to make sales calls very often.

Burn-out and F.E.A.R.

In today's business world you hear of people reaching burn-out in their careers. *Burn-out is simply a case where a person has lost sight of their goals.* Think of when you first started your job, you probably had an excitement about what was going to happen. As the job progressed you became more and more familiar with the process of doing the job correctly. As the job becomes mundane you lose the excitement and start on the path to burn-out.

> *Remember, the only difference between the rut, the groove and the grave is the depth you accept for yourself.*

To avoid burn out, keep looking for ways to make the job fun and exciting. We call this being **"constructively discontented"**. You are then always looking for ways to make the job more fun, more exciting, more profitable, easier, faster, better, etc.

Fear is something we all must face and conquer in our lives. Emerson said, *"Do the thing that you fear to do and the death of fear is certain"*. It may help to understand that fear stands for:

F – False

E – Evidence

A – Appearing

R – Real

There are two areas of fear we all have to deal with on our trip toward success. The Fear of Failure and the Fear of Success.

The definition of 'Fear of Failure': The conscious fear our inadequacies in certain areas will result in specific mistakes. Worry is the mind and ambition killer that stems directly from the Fear of Failure.

The definition of 'Fear of Success': The unconscious fear our success is coming too easily, hence we are a fraud. You can recognize the Fear of Success by the following statements: *"Everything is going too good, something bad is going to happen"! "I don't deserve this". Or "It's too good to be true"!*

Improvement Areas

Use **"Improvement Areas"** to keep on track in establishing and accomplishing goals. Improvement Areas are those areas in your life which may be unbalanced or just need some improvement. They can help you focus for everyday situations and move you into your major goal areas.

The following are some areas to help your goal setting process:

Customer relations	Visualization skills	Time management
Listening skills	Living areas	Self-confidence
Investments	Car	Vocabulary
Spelling skills	Income	Savings account
Record keeping	Wardrobe	Persuasiveness
Expand comfort zone	Product knowledge	Community involvement
Weight loss or gain	Ability to be myself	Ability to smile more often
Problem solving abilities	Concentration ability	Tact and diplomacy
Family time	Self-image	Sales skills
Enthusiasm	Perseverance	Memory skills
Self-worth	Courage	Physical fitness
Understanding others	Human relations skills	Verbal communication
Reading speed	Relationships	Empathy
Appreciation of others	Letter & memo writing skills	Administration skills
Daily sales calls	Pay compliments	Vacation time

Tips on Writing and Working on Goals

Over the years we have found certain keys to help people write their goals. Most people start to write their goals and find they do not write like they talk. They write in a more formal structure as if they had to defend them in the supreme court. Remember the Erdman KISS principle – **Keep It Super Simple**.

The following tips will help you write your goals:

1. Write them in pencil.

2. Make them a working document.

3. Write them in everyday language.

4. Keep them flexible - IT'S OK TO CHANGE.

5. Keep them positive.

6. Some goals will be maintenance goals.

7. Keep them in a three ring binder.

8. Keep them out where you will see them.

9. They can be drawings, etc.

10. Show them only to people of like mind.

11. Dream a little - dream a lot.

12. Reward yourself when results are achieved.

Action Verbs for Goal Statements

To reach a specific level of performance:

Achieve	Cut	Gain	Increase
Maintain	Obtain	Perform	Produce
Provide	Raise	Reach	Reduce
Save	Spend	Improve	Invest

To start something new:

Add	Conduct	Create	Complete
Develop	Design	Establish	Obtain
Plan	Produce	Provide	Start
Initiate			

Change something current:

Control	Change	Centralize	Correct
Decentralize	Decrease	Diversify	Enlarge
Eliminate	Gain	Improve	Increase
Modify	Reduce	Resolve	Solve
Strengthen	Stop	Update	

Continue something current:

Conduct	Continue	Hold	Maintain
Provide	Repeat	Accept	

Coordinate elements:

Announce	Assign	Communicate	Combine
Coordinate	Delegate	Discuss	Encourage
Gain	Inform	Involve	Join
Lead	Market	Participate	Promote
Publish	Separate	Support	

Investigate potential:

Analyze	Approve	Confirm	Determine
Evaluate	Examine	Experiment	Find
Identify	Recommend	Research	Review
Select	Study	Submit	Verify

Sample Goal Sheet

Improvement Areas:

_____

_____

_____

Long-term: (What can I do this year to move me towards my "Target Point"?)

_____

_____

_____

_____

Why is this goal important for me to accomplish?

_____

_____

_____

_____

Mid-Term: (Monthly or Quarterly)

_____

_____

_____

_____

Short-term: (Daily or Weekly)

_____

_____

_____

_____

It Is OK To Change!

It Couldn't Be Done

Edgar A. Guest

Somebody said that it couldn't be done
   but he with a chuckle replied,
That "maybe it couldn't", but he would be
   one who wouldn't say so until he tried.
So he buckled right in with a trace of
   a grin and if he worried he hid it.
He started to sing as he tackled the thing
   that couldn't be done, and he did it.

Somebody scoffed, "Oh, you'll never do
   that; at least no one has ever done it".
But he took off his coat and took off his hat
   and the first thing you know he'd begun it.
With a lift of his chin and a bit of
   a grin without any doubting or quiddit,
He started to sing as he tackled the thing
   That couldn't be done, and he did it.

There are thousands to tell you "it couldn't be
   done", there are thousands to prophesy failure;
There are thousands to point out to you, one
   by one, the dangers that wait to assail you.
But just buckle right in with a bit of a grin,
   just take off your coat and go to it;
Just start to sing as you tackle the thing
   that "couldn't be done", and you'll do it!

Quotes

"Nothing in this world can take the place of persistence. Talent will not; nothing is more common than unsuccessful men with talent. Genius will not; unrewarded genius is almost a proverb. Education will not; the world is full of educated derelicts. Persistence and persistence alone, always has and always will solve the problems of the human race".

Calvin Coolidge

"You must have long range goals to keep you from being frustrated by short range failures".

Charles C. Noble

"The unexamined life is not worth living".

Socrates

"We have nothing to fear but fear itself".

Franklin D. Roosevelt

When you were a child you faced many challenges and succeeded. You tried to walk until you could walk; you tried to run until you could run; you tried to talk until you could talk; You tried to read until you could read; and you tried to write until you could write. Why is it as an adult we put limitations on ourselves that make us less than what we were when we were children. Challenge yourself to win!

John C. Erdman

John C Erdman

Attitudes

The second step in *The C.A.R.E Principles* is to develop a positive confident attitude. A winning leader has a positive confident attitude about themselves, others and in the situations which they find themselves. They realize the subconscious mind has been recording everything they have seen, done, smelled, tasted, felt and thought since birth. All of these recordings are called our **"old memories"** and these memories play a large part in how we deal with any current situation.

Very simply, the mind functions on two levels, the **conscious** and the **subconscious**. **The conscious mind is your decision making tool; the subconscious mind is your computer or memory bank.** When you are faced with a decision, the conscious mind sends an order to the subconscious mind to play the memories on that subject. The conscious mind then makes a decision based on the feedback coming from the old memories and from the current data on the physical level.

To find out how long you have been building these old memories, take the formula of 24 x 365 x your age. This means you have been recording and learning 24 hours per day, 365 days per year, every year you have been alive.

24 x 365 = 8760 hours per year
8760 x your age = _____ hours
of old memories!

The subconscious mind records everything as fact and it does not perceive information in judgmental form. It simply records the thought or action as true. Because of this, it is possible to reprogram the mind to give you the results you desire. The subconscious mind is fertile ground.

You can control the information received into the subconscious mind with your self-talk. Realize, you spend most of your time alone with your thoughts and doing self-talk. Examples are driving your car, waiting in line at stores, using the washrooms, etc. You can do this either positively or negatively.

Positive self-talk opens the creative mind and frees the positive attitudes and mental resources needed to function in a winning manner. Negative self-talk locks up your mental resources, your attitudes and your actions. By turning your negative self-talk into positive self-talk and using positive affirmations you can take control of how you act and react to all situations and in all areas of your life.

Positive Self-Motivation

1. A motive is the positive or negative force within people that moves them into action in either a positive or negative way.

2. **Fear is the most powerful and destructive negative motivator** because it restricts, tightens, panics, forces, and defeats a person's ability to win and, often, even to try.

3. **Enthusiasm, excitement and desire are the strongest positive motivators** because they attract, reach, open, direct and encourage a person's ability to win.

4. You control your life either positively or negatively by the way you talk to yourself and the internal movies you allow yourself to run, that is, by your **self-talk**.

5. Winners always see the rewards of success in advance and always tell themselves *"I can", "I will"* and *"I want to";* they do not fear the penalties of failure.

6.	Losers always see the penalties of failure in advance and always tell themselves *"I can't"*, *"I won't"*, *"I have to"* and *"but, I tried"*; they fear both the rewards of success and the penalties of failure.

7.	Winners realize there is no such thing as a stress-free life and know how to respond positively to stress. They see stress or tension as energy and use it in the same way a rubber band uses tension to launch itself across the room They use it to their advantage rather than being controlled by it.

8.	You cannot move away from the reverse of an idea; your actions will be guided and controlled by your current dominant thoughts.

9.	What are your fears? Determine your fears and start to do the things you fear to do and the death of fear is absolutely certain. Remember, what we fear or resist we will attract, create or exaggerate. Action will minimize and ultimately eliminate fear.

10.	Positive self-motivation is a dissatisfaction with the status quo, or more simply, **a desire to change**.

11.	Positive self-motivation is a self-management skill which will move you in a positive direction. Remember: **"Life is a do-it-to-yourself project"**.

Negative Self-Talk

Desire and fear are the two greatest motivators. They propel or compel you to action, and make themselves visible through your thoughts and words. You are constantly talking - either to others or to yourself. Your life is affected - either positively or negatively - by your current dominant thoughts (your mental dialog or "self-talk"). Negative self-talk locks up your mental resources, your attitudes and your actions. Below is negative self-talk others say they use when thinking and talking to themselves. Check off the ones you say and **put a star** on the ones you say quite often to yourself.

1. ___ "There aren't enough hours in the day".

2. ___ "Someday I'll...".

3. ___ "I just don't know".

4. ___."If only...".

5. ___ "I have to...".

6. ___ "I'm not up to it".

7. ___ "I have a terrible memory".

8. ___ "It's the same old grind".

9. ___ "I'll never get that promotion".

10. ___ "It always happens to me".

11. ___ "I've had it"!

12. ___ "They always gets the breaks".

13. ___ "Everybody gives me their work to do".

14. ___ "I'm afraid".

15. ___ "I'll never make it".

16. ___ "I can't remember people's names".

17. ___ "I don't know where to begin".

18. ___ "I'm no good at this".

19. ___ "I blew it again".

20. ___ "I don't feel good".

21. ___ "I can't help it".

22. ___ "I don't think it'll work".

23. ___ "This looks really bad to me".

24. ___ "This place is a mess".

25. ___ "There's too much to do".

26. ___ "It's going to be one of those days".

27. ___ "I'm always the last one to know".

28. ___ "I can't get along with people".

29. ___ "No place to go in this dead end job".

30. ___ "I can't decide".

31. ___ "I'm worried".

32. ___ "Nobody loves me".

Establishing Positive Influences

Negative self-talk has a devastating effect on your life and work. On the other hand, positive self-talk has a freeing, expanding effect. There is a simple, two-step process for turning any negative thoughts into positive thoughts:

Step number one:
Make the decision to turn negative self-talk
into positive statements.

You can do this by:

1. Becoming aware of your own negative self-talk. Tell yourself that you will listen to what you are saying to or about yourself.
2. Turning your negative self-talk into positive self-talk.

Look at the negative self-talk you marked on the previous pages. Think about how you can turn these from negative to positive self-talk. For example, if you marked "I can't remember people's names", you could change it by saying "I can remember people's names with my excellent memory". On affirmations page you will find positive self-talk statements that correspond to the negative self-talk statements on the previous pages. Don't look ahead unless you're stuck!

Step number two:
Don't allow others to add negative self-talk to your thinking.

Negative self-talk is often a habit picked up from a parent, co-worker or a friend. For example, a person might state, "My mother told me I had a terrible memory". She would say, "You'd forget your head if it wasn't attached to your body"!

The next time someone offers you some of their negative statements, don't agree mentally with them. Instead, affirm positive self-talk. Here are some negative statements others may impose on you. What positive self-talk can you use to keep this kind of conversation from affecting you negatively?

"Sure is a lousy day, isn't it"?

"I don't trust them, do you"?

"I don't think it will work, do you"?

"This company doesn't care about us"?

"He really made a mess of it, didn't he"?

When someone states something negatively and expects a response from you, you have three choices:

1. You can ignore the comment and say nothing.
2. You can agree with the comment.
3. You can turn it around and help the person see the positive side of the situation.

Guidelines for Using Positive Self-Talk

1. **Use personal pronouns.** Words such as "I", "my", "mine" and "me" will personalize your self-talk and will help you internalize it.

Ineffective Self-Talk	Effective Self-Talk
"People are fun to be around".	**"I enjoy being around people".**
"Time is money".	**"I am well organized and efficient".**

2. **Keep your positive self-talk in the present tense.** Referring to the past or future dilutes the impact of your self-talk.

Ineffective Self-Talk	Effective Self-Talk
"Someday I'll be successful".	**"I am successful".**
"I am better disciplined than I was".	**"I am well disciplined".**

3. **Direct your positive self-talk toward what you desire, not away from what you don't want.** You want to focus your current dominant thought on your desires, not your dislikes.

Ineffective Self-Talk	Effective Self-Talk
"I can quit smoking".	"I am in control of my habits".
"I will lose 20 pounds".	"I weigh a slim, trim _____ pounds".
"I won't worry anymore".	"I am a confident, optimistic person".

4. **Keep your self-talk noncompetitive, rather than comparing yourself with others.**

Ineffective Self-Talk	Effective Self-Talk
"I will become president before he (or she) does".	"I am president, fully capable of fulfilling my responsibilities".

Positive Quick Affirmations

You can also use quick affirmations to help in any situation. One of the most effective techniques to help cancel out the negative thoughts or words is the "**delete, delete**" statement. When a negative statement is made to you or you think or say a negative statement, immediately say or think **"delete, delete"**, then say or think a positive statement several times. This puts the positive statement into the subconscious mind instead of the negative one.

Use these with the "delete, delete" statement:

Happiness, I am.	Abundant, I am.
Rich, I am.	Energy, I am.
Patience, I am.	Prosperity, I am.
Forgiveness, I am.	Spiritual, I am.
Loving, I am.	Health, I am.
Slim, I am.	Peace, I am.

Affirmations

Every day in every way, I'm getting better and better!
Today I am bright, cheerful and happy! Streams of power
flow through my veins! All is well!

I believe in myself! I am! I can! I will! I do!

If it is to be, it is up to me! I act, not react!

I take action now!

I'm Terrific, I'm Tremendous, When I'm being me, I'm
Stupendous!

Positive Self-Talk

Sometimes the subconscious mind may want to reject a positive statement is not true. If when you make a positive statement yourself and it feels false to you or you have a negative internal response to it like *"when pigs fly"* or *"yeah right, Not"*, try adding, *"I am now becoming..."*. As is *"I am now becoming more confident every day"*, or *"I am practicing remembering names"*. Softening the statement can make it more plausible to the subconscious and it will be more likely to accept the positive statement:

1. "I have all the time I need".

2. "I am...".

3. "I make great decisions".

4. "It is great that...".

5. "I want to...".

6. "I'm always ready".

7. "I have a wonderful memory".

8. "I am always successful".

9. "I am the Sales Manager".

10. "Good things always happen to me".

11. "I've just begun"!

12. "I make the breaks work for me".

13. "Everybody trusts me".

14. "I am confident".

15. "I always win".

16. "I can remember people's names".

17. "I always start at the right place".

18. "I'm good at this".

19. "I won again".

20. "I feel good".

21. "I can help".

22. "I know it will work".

23. "This looks really great to me".

24. "This place is in order".

25. "Everything is done in the right time".

26. "This is one of those great days".

27. "I am always the first to know".

28. "I get along with everybody".

29. "I make opportunity happen for me".

30. "I can always decide".

31. "I'm positive".

32. "Everybody loves me".

Recognizing Your Success Patterns

In our lives we do many successful things we have a tendency to forget about. On the following page use the spaces to write down some of the things you feel good about. These are your success patterns and by recalling them you can start to see you are a successful person.

Grade School Years:

_____

_____

_____

High School Years:

_____

_____

_____

College, Other Educational Schools, and Military Years:

_____

_____

_____

Family Experiences:

_____

_____

_____

Work Experience:

_____

_____

_____

Other Experiences:

_____

_____

_____

After looking at your success patterns this way, write a brief statement about who you are and how you feel about yourself:

_____

_____

_____

EGO Walls

These are the items you would put up on your **"ego"** wall. Always be looking for items which make you feel good about yourself and put these up on the "ego" wall. Could be a news clipping, a thank you card, a beautiful picture, or a trophy, etc. Then when you are falling into a negative downer, you just look at the wall and you will start to feel good about yourself, realizing you are indeed a successful person.

Current Dominant Thought

You move in the direction of what you are thinking of most. This is your current dominant thought. It is very important for you to focus your attention and concentrate your thoughts (your positive self-talk) on the condition you want to achieve, rather than attempt to move away from what you fear or don't want. Simply stated, winners focus on the final results rather than on the problems that must be overcome to achieve the results.

The first step in controlling your dominant thoughts is to ask yourself, "what do I really want"? If I could make things happen right now, what could I achieve within my work setting?

Listed below are things people say they want. Perhaps these will be dominant thought starters for you. Check the ones you would like to achieve. Then add other dominate thoughts specifically for you. Disregard any fear of failure. Dream.

What do I really want?

___ become more self-confident

___ remember people's names

___ stop smoking

___ develop my career

___ be appreciated for my work

___ travel the country/world

___ earn more money

___ receive a promotion

___ communicate effectively

___ hold effective meetings

___ lose weight

___ have more energy

___ develop financial security

___ relax at will

___ manage time better

___ eat more nutritious foods

_____ overcome worry

_____ be more enthusiastic

_____ people like & respect me

_____ feel comfortable in a crowd

others:

_____

_____

_____

_____

Writing Affirmations

The first thing you must do is to take a **"Profit and Loss"** statement on yourself. This will show how you perceive yourself internally. List some things you like about yourself and some things you would like to change about yourself.

Likes	**Dislikes**
_____	_____
_____	_____
_____	_____
_____	_____
_____	_____

By writing affirmations to change the things we do not like, we can program the subconscious to make the changes happen. The formula to write an affirmation is simple and fun to do. Remember the subconscious mind does not know when you are kidding or lying to it. The formula is a two-step process:

1. *Tell yourself how good you are.*
2. *Remind yourself of your past successes.*

When you tell yourself how good you are in an area where the old memories say you are not very good, you are starting to reprogram that area. Your conscious mind may say, "Who are you trying to kid"? However, the subconscious mind just records that you are good in that area. **The more times you reprogram the subconscious, the more good feedback you will receive from it.** When you remind yourself of past successes, you are just amplifying the effect. You do not have to have any past success, just make some up. This is where you can have some real creative fun. Think of the times when things didn't work out and now change them into positive experiences. **Take the thing you want to do and make it your most recent past success.**

Write down an affirmation in the space provided.

Attitude to change: _____

Step 1 (How good you are): _____

_____

_____

_____

Step 2 (Past successes): _____

_____

_____

_____

_____

Repeat out loud, this and any other affirmations you are working on, at least twice per day. Once in the morning upon rising and again just before you go to bed at night. It takes approximately twenty-one days to change a habit or attitude. You should do a profit and loss statement at least once per quarter. Make a list of everything you like about yourself and everything you do not like about yourself. Then pick several to work on for the next quarter.

Imaging

Mental Rehearsal

Imaging the thing you are about to do in a positive manner will start you on the road to success. When we speak of imaging, we are talking about seeing what you are about to do, in the mind's eye. This does the same thing as your affirmations. Any time you use self-talk in any form you are dealing with the subconscious mind and can begin to program new memories or reprogram the old memories.

An example of imaging is what many top professional speakers do when they accept a speaking assignment. They often ask to be sent a picture of the room where they will be speaking and then use this picture in the image they create in their mind. They see the room filled to capacity and the people responding the way the speaker wants them to respond. Use all of your mind's senses (that make sense): the mind's eye, the mind's nose, the mind's ear, the mind's taste and the mind's touch.

Many people use negative imaging without realizing it. Just before they do something they begin to create disaster moves in their mind, to think of all the objections and all of the reasons why the project won't work. Then they start to think of how to manipulate the situation so it might work. By the time they get face to face with the person or project they have forgotten any professionalism they might have had and it becomes a losing situation.

Positive imaging like positive self-talk and positive affirmations, puts you on target to success. Always look for the good in any situation then begin to image good happening right now. With practice you can create positive experiences anytime and anywhere.

Poems

The following poems are a bit outdated in the language they use but the meaning rings true today as much as it did when they were written. So excuse the use of the words and let them speak to your heart.

The World Is Mine

Dot Aaron

Today, upon a bus, I saw a lovely girl with golden hair. I envied her, she seemed so gay, and wished I were as fair. When suddenly she rose to leave, I saw her hobble down the aisle; She had one leg, and wore a crutch, and as she passed -- a smile. O God, forgive me when I whine. I have two legs. The world is mine.

And then I stopped to buy some sweets, the lad who sold them had such charm. I talked with him -- he seemed so glad if I were late 'twould do no harm. And as I left, he said to me, "I thank you. You have been so kind. It's nice to talk with folks like you. You see," he said, "I'm blind". O God, forgive me when I whine. I have two eyes. The world is mine.

Later, walking down the street, I saw a child with eyes of blue. He stood and watched the others play; it seemed he knew not what to do. I stopped a moment, then I said, "Why don't you join the others, dear"? He looked ahead without a word, and then I knew -- he could not hear. O God, forgive me when I whine. I have two ears. The world is mine.

With legs to take me where I'd go -- with eyes to see the sunset's glow -- with ears to hear what I would know -- O God, forgive me when I whine. I'm blessed indeed. The world is mine!

Poem For Women

Dr. Denis Waitley

Mirror, mirror on my wall
    What's the meaning of it all?
Is there something more to life
    Than to be his loving wife?

Yes I love my children dearly
    But they'll grow up and come by yearly.
Dare I yearn for something more
    Than to cook and wax the floor?

What about the needs I feel
    Are my dreams considered real?
What about an education
    A voice to shape the nation.

I'm not angry or rebelling
  But there's something strong and compelling.
Is my destined heritage a twofold page
  Of a girlie magazine, a sexy pin-up queen.

I've got a body and a soul,
  I've got a mind, I've got a goal.
I'd like to learn, I'd like to teach,
  I'd like to earn, I'd like to reach,
I'd like to fly from my cocoon,
  Put my footsteps on the moon.

The world's a better place
  With my special female grace.
I don't want to be a man,
  I love the woman that I am.

But mirror, mirror on my wall
  Help me hear my inner call
All I've ever hoped to be is free
  To be that person -- Me.

Poem For Men

Dr. Denis Waitley

Crystal ball, oh, crystal ball

Will my empire rise and fall

Like the Roman legion must

Ash to ash and dust to dust?

Is there something more to life than to build it for my wife

And to give our children more than their parents had before.

I go to work, I earn the bread, I watch T.V. and I go to bed,

And sunrise, sunset year to year before I know it, winter's here.

But it's not a scrimmage or a practice game

And there's no martyr's hall of fame.

Time, the speedster, takes its toll,

And everyday's the super bowl.

Losers live in classic style,

That never world called, "Someday I'll".

They blame bad luck each time they lose

And hide it with sickness, drugs and booze.

And losing is a habit and so is winning,

If I'm going to change, I'll start beginning

To live each day as if my last

Not in the future, not in the past.

I'll dream it now, I'll plan it now,

I'll want it now, I'll do it now.

I'll close my eyes and truly see

The person I'd most like to be.

Mirror, mirror, crystal ball,

Help me hear my inner call.

I think I can, I know I can

Become my greatest coach and fan.

And I love myself but I'll give away

All the love I can today.

And I think I can and I know I can

Become the most uncommon man.

Quotes

Ideals

William James

As you think, you travel; and as you love, you attract. You are today where your thoughts have brought you, you will be tomorrow where your thoughts take you. You cannot escape the results of your thoughts, but you can endure and learn, can accept and be glad. You will realize the vision (not the idle wish) of your heart be it base or beautiful, or a mixture of both, for you will always gravitate towards that which you, secretly, must love. Into your thoughts you will receive that which you earn; no more, no less. Whatever your present environment may be, you will fall, remain, or rise with your thoughts, your visions, your ideals. You will become as small as your controlling desire; as great as your dominant aspiration.

It's not the size of the dog in the fight, but the size of the fight in the dog.

Tom Barrett

God, grant me the serenity to accept the
things I cannot change.
The courage to change the things I can.
And the wisdom to know the difference.

Relationships

The third step in *The C.A.R.E Principles* is to build solid, positive relationships with everyone you contact. This means not only your family and friends, but also your co-workers, your boss, the neighbors and the person who just stops you on the street to ask for the time.

Have you ever wondered why relationships with other people are so difficult at times? Every time you come into contact with another person you are really dealing with the three different personalities:

1. *Who they think they are.*
2. *Who they really are.*
3. *Who they become by dealing with us.*

Many people have masks they wear in different situations and they assume the identity of the mask. You can call this identity their **"perceived truth"**, this is who they think they are, but deep down inside they are who they really are. Sometimes it is so well buried they don't even know who the person really is.

You become a changed identity because of your dealings with someone else. This change can be very slight or very large depending on the contact. Also you can be changed from a positive person into a negative person or vice versa by a positive or negative contact.

There is an old Chinese proverb that says it nicely:

If there is righteousness in the heart, there will be beauty in the character. If there is beauty in the character, there will be harmony in the home. If there is harmony in the home, there will be order in the nation. When there is order in the nation, there will be peace in the world.

The Four Ways of Judgment

There are four ways in which you judge and are judged by other people. These four ways can also produce positive or negative results. Because you are reading people every time you are in contact with them, you assume that you can tell all about a person just by looking at and listening to them. You are not always correct in your assumptions and most of the time feel offended if someone judges you incorrectly. Yet these four values are used by everybody, even though we know they are not just or fair.

The four ways are:

1. *How one looks.*
2. *What one says.*
3. *How one says it.*
4. *How one treats people.*

How one looks. In the world of business you make certain assumptions of who a person is by the way they are dressed and by the way they carry themselves. A person who is dressed for success and walks with an air of confidence is automatically believed to be successful and someone you can trust for their abilities. Likewise you assume someone not dressed well or who carries an air of nervousness is someone you cannot trust.

What one says. Your vocabulary tells other people how to assume your education level and your class level. People with higher education or a higher class upbringing usually have a better or richer vocabulary. One way to increase your vocabulary is to use a list of new words until you have installed them in your mind and can use them easily. Such lists can be found on-line (search for "daily vocabulary"), on some daily calendars, newspapers or in some of the magazines we buy regularly. Readers Digest for example has a new list every month with pronunciations and meanings for each word. This is an area where we all can set goals and reach new potentials.

How one says it. Your voice inflection says different things for the same words. People make the assumption of what you are saying based on the inflection in your voice. If you are going to really advance your career you will have to do something most people never do. That is to deliberately train yourself on how to use your voice more effectively. In order to train your voice you must use a voice recorder and practice, practice, practice.

Voice Inflection Exercise

To illustrate the use of voice inflection we use a seven word statement and have seven different meanings for the statement.

"I never said he stole the money".

Each time you say it, put the emphasis on a different word. By using your voice inflection you change the meaning of the statement each time. Without any emphasis it is just a factual statement. But with emphasis:

1. "**I** never said he stole the money". (Assumption: it was said, by someone else.)

2. "I **never** said he stole the money". (Assumption: a vigorous denial that I said it.)

3. "I never **said** he stole the money". (Assumption: I might have implied it, but I didn't say it.)

4. "I never said **he** stole the money". (Assumption: someone else stole the money.)

5. "I never said he **stole** the money". (Assumption: he may have "borrowed" it, but he didn't actually steal it.)

6. "I never said he stole **the** money". (Assumption: he may have stolen some money, but not the money.)

7. "I never said he stole the **money**". (Assumption: he may have stolen something else, but not money.)

How one treats people. By the use of human relation concepts we can influence those around us. We make certain assumptions about people by watching how they treat those around them.

Earning Trust

"Do I trust people"? Others may ask many questions about you, but this is a key one. Trust lies at the root of building good interpersonal relations. Research into human relations proves that if trust is present, weaknesses tend to be overlooked and mistakes tolerated. Some people are trusted, and some are not, it depends on how they behave. Trust is grounded in four very concrete and specific behaviors: **Acceptance, Integrity, Openness, Reliability**. The presence of these four behaviors lead others to say: "I trust you". If you put these four behaviors into practice, you'll be trusted. If you don't, you won't. Simple as that. Let's look at each of the four in turn, to get the whole picture.

1. Trust requires **acceptance**. If I sense you accept me as a person, I'll trust you. That means I must sense that you feel it's OK for me to be me, you don't pass judgment on me, you don't put me down and you don't treat me as an "it" by trying to manipulate me, treat me as an inferior or by just criticizing me. You accept me as an individual with my thoughts, feelings, interests, differences and my imperfections. You don't have to agree with me, but you do have to accept me. If I sense you don't accept me, I won't trust you, because I'll wonder if you are trying to use me, or deal with me only as a means to your ends. If you behave in an accepting manner by taking me as I am, treating me as a worthwhile person, showing respect for my

personhood and not judging me, then your behavior will lead me toward trusting you. *Acceptance is necessary to earn trust.*

2. Trust requires **integrity**. If I sense you are being straight forward with me, I'll trust you. That means I must see you as being honest with me. I must perceive that you mean what you say and say what you mean; that's having integrity. If I sense that you are telling me one thing and feeling the opposite, trust goes down. If I don't see and feel your integrity, I won't trust you, because I'll be in doubt about what you really mean. Feeling that I can't count on you to tell me the truth. If you behave in a honest way, saying what you mean and meaning what you say, then your behavior will lead me toward trusting you. *Integrity is necessary to earn trust.*

3. Trust requires **openness**. If I sense you are being open with me, I'll trust you. That means I must feel that you are letting me in on what you know about the matter at hand, at least the essentials. I must perceive that you are willing to let me know what affects me; that's being open. If I sense you are keeping important things to yourself or that you have a hidden agenda, trust goes down and you become less believable to me. If you behave in an open way, share information with me and tell me what you have in mind, then your behavior will lead me toward trusting you. *Openness is necessary to earn trust.*

4. Trust requires **reliability**. If I sense you are dependable, I'll trust you. That means you do what you say you'll do. If you make a promise, you'll keep it. If you say you'll take care of something, you'll take care of it. If you say you'll be somewhere, you'll be there. I must have the experience that you take your agreements seriously, you are a person of your word; that's being reliable. If I see you making promises you don't keep and if you say you won't do a certain thing, then you do it, trust goes down. If you behave in a reliable way and if I can bank on your dependability, then your behavior will lead me toward trusting you. *Reliability is necessary to earn trust.*

Trust is the cornerstone for building ongoing, lasting relationships. Trust is earned, it's not a gift. Others don't trust you just because you tell them you can be trusted. You earn trust by your behavior, and that takes time. *You earn it if you behave with acceptance, integrity, openness and reliability.*

The following is a list of nine basic human relation concepts and one special concept we can use to increase the influence we have with people and help others feel good about themselves.

A Closer Look at Human Relation Concepts

Human Relations Concept List

1. Use the "Golden Rule". Do unto others as you would have them do unto you.

2. Smile. Always have a cheerful countenance.

3. Make the other person feel important.

4. Train your memory to recall important items.

5. Be a good listener.

6. Become a sparkling conversationalist.

7. Call attention to people's mistakes indirectly.

8. Motivate people in terms of their interests, benefits and satisfaction.

9. Write letters of appreciation.

10. Hugs.

1. Use the Golden Rule.

Probably the most often talked about yet least used human relation concept is the "Golden Rule". ***"Do onto others as you would have them do onto you".*** In other words, treat everyone as a special person. There are approximately six billion people on this earth and no two are alike. Everyone is unique and each has an interesting story to tell if you are willing to listen.

Peter Marshall, Chaplain of the U.S. Senate in the 1950's, said *"Treat every person as if their heart is breaking, because it probably is".* Every person's problems are to them the most important events happening to them at the moment. By remembering this, you will treat them in a better light than they might otherwise warrant. To have empathy you must walk in the other person's shoes at least temporarily. You will start to understand them better when you look at the problem from their point of view. Remember what we really want is empathy from other people, not their sympathy. What you give out you will receive back. So make sure you give out positive words and feelings, not negative words and feelings.

2. Smile.
Always have a cheerful countenance.

A very simple human relation concept that will help you in almost any situation is a smile. Smiling is easy to do and does not cost you anything to give away. Dr. Denis Waitley puts it nicely, "Winners display a simple, radiating charm. They project a warm glow that comes from the inside outward. Most importantly, self-esteem is transmitted with a smile, which is the universal language that opens doors, melts defenses and saves a thousand words. *A smile is the light in your window that tells others there is a caring, sharing person inside*".

Starting today, challenge yourself to smile and say **"hello"** first to each person you meet. As you walk down the street, smile at everyone and watch how many people smile back at you. You will feel good about yourself and give other people an opportunity to share the feeling.

When you talk on the phone, smile; it changes the muscles in the face and throat, people will hear the smile coming through the phone. Put a small mirror by your phone with a label on it saying, "Would I want to talk to someone who looks like this"? When your answer is "yes", you can answer the call or make your call. If you use a cell phone put the mirror where you will see it.

3. Make the other person feel important.

Emerson said, "Every man I meet is in some way my superior; and in that I can learn of him". William James, the father of modern American psychology, stated, "The deepest principle in human nature is the craving to be appreciated". If you know each person can indeed teach you something and they also have a need to be appreciated, you can certainly make them feel important by showing them you feel this way. To help you remember this, picture a sign hanging around everyone's neck saying, **"Make me feel important"**!

Pay honest and sincere compliments.

Paying honest and sincere compliments is one of the best ways to give out good, positive feelings to other people. Giving a compliment to someone builds their self-esteem and cements the relationship into positive ground. William James said, **"The deepest principle in human nature is the craving to be appreciated"**.

Always be looking for the good in people and then tell them the good you see in them. Use the **T.A.P.** formula to help you become aware of material for compliments. TAP stands for:

T = Things

A = Accomplishments

P = Personality Traits

The best formula to use when paying compliments is:

1. *Tell the person what you like.*
2. *Tell them why you like it.*
3. *Ask them an open-ended question about it.*

When you tell a person what and why you like something, it takes you out of flattery and gives them a sincere compliment. To ask the open-ended question shows them you really do care.

When asking open-ended questions, remember Rudyard Kipling's poem:

I keep six honest serving men
they taught me all I knew,
their names are What, Why,
When, How, Where and Who.

If you need to get some information from another person you can start with a compliment called, **"People Builders"**. People builders start out saying, *"Someone with your ...."*.

Some of the things to use in people builders are:

Background	Courtesy	Decisiveness
Education	Efficiency	Experience
Flexibility	Humor	Knowledge
Neatness	Physical Fitness	Taste

Use praise at every opportunity.

Charles Schwab, (whom Andrew Carnegie paid one million dollars per year salary), said, "There is nothing else that so kills the ambitions of a person as criticisms from their superiors. I never criticize anyone. I believe in giving a person incentive to work. So I am anxious to praise, but loath to find fault. *If I like anything, I am hearty in my approbation and lavish in my praise*".

In the book "The One Minute Manager", Spencer Johnson and Kenneth Blanchard state the motto they use is, *"Help people reach their potential, catch them doing something right"*. When they catch someone doing things even approximately right, they praise them. You need to start watching people. Catch them doing things right. Then be *"hearty in your approbation and lavish in your praise"*.

Most people see other people for their weaknesses instead of their strengths. Good human relations demand we look at others' strengths and then let them know we see those qualities. Sometimes we are the only ones who see these qualities in them. They may be so accustomed to hearing that they are too slow, too old, too young, too dumb, only a male, only a female, etc. that they have indeed become these things. When we let others know we expect them to live and work up to their potentials, they will do everything in their power to do so.

4. Train your memory to recall important items.

There is no such thing as a good or bad memory, only a trained or untrained memory. Your mind thinks in pictures not in words. To remember anything, build a picture of the item and then stack the pictures together. You can do this with a list of grocery items, a things to do list, a sales demonstration, a speech you have to give, people's names, a work process, etc. You need to make your pictures as colorful and crazy as possible, as this will help lock them in your mind. You can use the **A.C.E. Formula:**

> *A = Action*
> *C = Color*
> *E = Exaggeration*

Remember people's names. Use them at every opportunity.

By developing your memory you will be able to remember people's names and any other important things you have to do. Your mind thinks in pictures, so when you're trying to remember something, you have to get a good picture of the item in your mind's eye. Have you ever wondered why you can remember someone's face but not the name? It's because you see the picture of the face but you did not put the person's name in the picture. Dale Carnegie said, *"Remember a person's name is to them the sweetest and most important sound in any language"*.

Most people are taught as children what to do when they come to a railroad crossing. A child is instructed to **Stop**, **Look**, **Listen**, and then **Proceed**. You use the same steps when beginning to train your memory on how to remember people's names. You must Stop what you are thinking about; Look at the person; Listen for the name; and then Proceed to use the name at every opportunity. All this takes time, but as Emerson said, *"Good manners are made up of petty sacrifices"*.

You can further develop this technique by using the I.R.A. Formula.

I = Impression   R = Repetition   A = Association

5. Be a good listener.

Listening skills will help improve your conversations and your relationships. Most people hear what the other person is saying without really listening. To uncover what people want, spend less time talking and more time **listening.** The best actors and the most effective salespeople traditionally have not been great talkers; they have been good listeners.

When you listen your way in,
you don't have to talk your way out.

Listening is really an indication of interest in the person. It takes real interest to listen effectively despite distractions such as time pressure, noise, and language barriers. Surprisingly, one of the most important skills for good listening is *asking questions.* Asking questions shows your interest in the person and forces you to listen carefully because you cannot ask good questions if you are not listening. Asking questions also keeps you from talking too much and helps you confirm what the person has said. You can actually "feel" when you are doing a good job of listening.

Suggestions for more effective listening.

1. **Give the speaker your full attention with your eyes and body.** Eye contact helps you stay tuned-in to the person and gives the impression that the person has your full attention.

2. **Ask people to speak up or slow down if necessary.** You cannot understand what you cannot hear.

3. **Don't interrupt.** Force yourself to hear fully what the other person is saying or you may miss the key point.

4. **Avoid using "yes, but . . ."** It gives the speaker the feeling that you were not listening - that you were thinking of your reply.

5. **Repeat in your own words your understanding of what the person has said**, including what you understand their feelings to be. Keep key phrases in the same order as the person that spoke them. Example, *"my new red car"* encodes differently in the brain then *"my new car is red"*. The person is more likely to feel heard if you repeat back *"what make is your new red car"*, then *"what make is your new car"* Ask the person if your understanding is correct.

6. **By nodding and commenting to encourage the person, you can keep the person talking.**

7. **Put yourself in the other person's place and be aware of how he or she seems to feel.**

Confirm messages

Listening is not enough. It is too easy to jump to incorrect conclusions or to misinterpret the other person's message. That is why it is important to **confirm**, or check your understanding of messages. There are no easy ways to confirm messages. You can confirm the message you received by an open-ended question, by paraphrasing ... repeating what has been said in your own words.

Confirming Skills

In your mind, you have plenty of time to listen and question what the other person is really saying. Your mind can hear and comprehend a minimum of 600 words per minute; a fast talking person can reach only about 150 words per minute. Use this extra time to really listen to and confirm the meaning and words that are being said.

Most people hear what the other person is saying without really listening. The following list contains techniques to use to develop your confirming skills:

1. Concentration (become fascinated).

2. Anticipate what is to be said.

3. Mentally summarize what has been said.

4. Look for the point people are trying to make.

5. Listen between the lines.

6. Paraphrase statements to clarify them.

7. Weigh the evidence by mentally questioning it:

    A. What point are they trying to make?

    B. Am I getting the facts?

    C. Am I getting the truth?

    D. Am I getting the whole truth?

    E. What does this really mean?

    F. How did they mean that?

    G. Why do they feel that way?

6. Become a sparkling conversationalist.

When you become a sparkling conversationalist it means you have the ability to draw the other person out of their shell and communicate effectively with them. The other person will be doing most of the talking and we should make it a point to get the person talking about something in which they are interested. In the following stack are the pictures that will help you become a sparkling conversationalist. Mentally see the pictures described:

On the bottom is a large jeweled **crown** with an eight foot **ear** sticking out of the top. To the left of the ear is a **house**. Coming out of the top of the house is a **ruler**. Bumping into the ruler is a **work glove** holding a **wooden Indian**. On top of the wooden Indian there is a **mountain** full of **peaks** and **valleys**. To the right of the mountain is a **car, plane and train**. Just above the car, plane and train is a **soccer ball**. Right in the middle of it all is a bright shining **light bulb**.

The items in the stack stand for your attitude and the questions to ask to engage an open conversation with the other person.

Crown =	**An attitude of respect.**
Ear =	**Listen to the other person.**
House =	**"Where do you live"?**
Work glove =	**"What do you do for a living (work)"?**
Wooden Indian =	**"*How* did you get into that line of work"?**
Mountain peaks =	**"Share with me some of the accomplishments you have had that make you successful today"?**
Mountain valleys =	**"Share with me some of the challenges you have had that make you successful today"?**
Car, plane & train=	**"Do you travel"?**
Soccer ball =	**"What do you do for recreation"?**
Light bulb =	**"What do you think of ...."?**

Keep open channels of communications.

Just being a sparkling conversationalist and asking questions is not enough to keep the channels of communications open. You have to look at and understand the road blocks to communication and how to overcome these road blocks.

Road blocks to communications

A. **Prejudice** -- Webster's New World Dictionary: 1.] A judgment or opinion formed before the facts are known; preconceived idea, favorable or, more usually, unfavorable. 2.] A judgment or opinion held in disregard of the facts that contradict it; unreasonable bias.

B. **Semantic Differences** -- Webster's New World Dictionary: Semantic, of or pertaining to meaning, especially meaning in language. You must become aware of feelings, assumptions, viewpoints and attitudes.

C. **Lack Of Confidence** -- Book of Lists: Interviewing 3,000 people across the nation about their greatest fear, number one was speaking in public and number seven was death. More people would rather die than speak in public.

D. **Speaking Over The Head Of The Listener** -- Speaking in "buzz" words. Using a $10.00 word for a $2.00 statement.

E. **Understanding But Not Accepting What Is Said** -- "I know you think you heard what I said, but I'm not sure what you understood is what I meant."

F. **Hearing But Not Listening** -- We can hear and understand at the rate of 600 words per minute minimum, while we can only speak at a rate of 100 to 150 words per minute maximum.

G. **Lack Of Trust** -- From the beginning many people do not believe they will get a fair hearing. "No one ever believes me, so why should I try to communicate with anyone"?

H. **Non-Verbal Communications** -- The body language is saying something different than what is being said verbally.

Overcoming the road blocks to communications

A. **Empathy** -- Webster's New World Dictionary: The projection of one's own personality into the personality of another in order to understand them better; Ability to share in another's emotions or feelings.

B. **Realistically Understanding The Other Person's Differences** -- What kind of state of mind is the other person in; what kind of background do they have, etc.

C. **Words That Are Understood By All** -- Use the KISS Formula, Keep It Super Simple. When all concerned can understand what you are saying your communications will be on target.

D. **Speak Clearly** -- Do not slur or mumble words, speak loud enough for all to hear clearly.

E. **Be Aware Of Non-Verbal Signals** -- Body language and what it is saying to you. Body language is becoming more of an exact science all the time, and it is something you should read about and study if you want to really open clear communications.

F. **Analyze And Evaluate The Tone Of Voice** -- Is what they are saying matching the tone and meaning in their voice? Does the body language also confirm voice tone and meaning? Rate or pace of the speech is important and you must match that rate or pace to get in step with the other person. Once you are in step with the other person you can pick the pace up or slow it down, depending on the situation

G. **Start Listening When The Other Person Starts Talking**
Immediately starting to listen is the only way to be able to really hear what is being said. If you do not start listening immediately you will miss some of what the person is saying and the part you miss could be the real statement.

Ask questions instead of giving orders

No one likes to take orders from anyone. We have been around people who give orders and never listen to anyone else's opinion. It is no fun to be around people like that. **A good leader will give suggestions and ask for input from their people.** They are always encouraging their people to try new ways of doing things and overlook or gently correct the occasional mistake. This way you will always get feedback from your people and your relationships will improve.

7. Call attention to people's mistakes indirectly.

When you point out other people's mistakes directly you just make them stand behind their decision even harder. One of the best ways to show or talk about mistakes is to point out the mistakes you've made first. This lets the other person realize we are not perfect and there is always room for improvement.

Remember the largest room in the world is the room for self-improvement.

Do not argue. Not argue, you might say, then how can I get my point across? Well, a misunderstanding is never ended by an argument; rather by tact, diplomacy, conciliation, and an empathic desire to see the other person's point of view. There is an old saying that goes: "**A man convinced against his will is of the same opinion still**".

Ben Franklin said, "If you argue and rankle and contradict, you may achieve a victory sometimes; but it will be an empty victory because you will never get your opponent's good will".

When you are working on remembering this human relation concept it may help to see the grave marker of a Mr. William Jay in your mind.

Here lies the body of William Jay,
Who died maintaining his right of way;
He was right, dead right, as he sped along,
But he's just as dead as if he were wrong.

You may be right in the argument, but as far as changing anyone's mind, you might as well be wrong. **When you are wrong, admit it.** If you want to win people to your way of thinking, admit it when you're wrong and do it quickly. When admitting your mistakes you are showing other people you are big enough to realize your faults. This is not very easy to do because your ego gets in the way when you want to let others know you're not perfect.

Just think back to your last argument where you were in the wrong. Did you stop arguing the moment you realized you were wrong or did you just keep on arguing and maybe admit it later? Try admitting it when you are wrong and see how good you feel and how the other people will respond to you.

8. Motivate people in terms of their interests, benefits and satisfaction.

The road to a person's heart is to talk to them about the things they treasure the most. Probably the best way to remember this is the **W.II.F.M. Formula**:

$$W = \textit{What's}$$
$$II = \textit{In It}$$
$$F = \textit{For}$$
$$M = \textit{Me}$$

From now on see the letters W.II.F.M. branded on the other person's forehead. These letters can also stand for the call letters of the world's largest radio station, because everyone is always listening to it. Always think of these letters and what they stand for before you begin talking. You will be reaching the other person's emotional drives and these are the drives that motivate all people.

Dramatize your ideas.

If you want to get your point across to someone else, dramatize it. The use of drama and showmanship in selling, advertising and speaking are the keys to success. By dramatizing your ideas you are not just telling someone cold, hard facts but are telling them a story full of color and excitement. People do everything emotionally and justify it logically. Dramatize the points you want to make and you appeal to the emotions.

Challenge people to excel.

Charles Schwab said, "The way to get things done is to stimulate competition. I do not mean in a sordid, money getting way, but in the desire to excel". The story is told of Schwab going to a steel mill that was down on production. While talking to the manager about what had been done to stimulate the workers to greater production, the shift changed. Schwab asked one of the leaving men how many heats had been made that day. The reply was "6", which Schwab chalked on the floor. The night shift finding out what the six represented, proceeded to do "7" heats and mark that on the floor. The day shift then did "10" heats and so on until the mill was one of the best in the business.

If you want to help people reach greater potential, offer them a challenge that brings out their desire to excel.

9. Write letters of appreciation.

Have you ever received an expression of appreciation from someone? Or have you received a written letter of appreciation? If so, how did you feel about yourself and the person who sent it to you? Do you still have the letter and maybe refer to it once in a while? Most people are well meaning and give lip service to writing letters of appreciation but never seem to get around to writing or sending them.

Think for a moment of three people in your life who you appreciate for some reason (alive, please). It may be a spouse, a child, a teacher or a friend, etc. Write their names on the following lines.

1. _____

2. _____

3. _____

Circle one of the names you have just listed and on a separate piece of paper write a letter of appreciation to the person. If you need help starting the letter you can use the following opening lines:

"I am reading a book where the reader was asked to write a letter of appreciation to one special person. I choose you because ....".

Assuming you never heard back from this person, how do you feel about what you have just done? Would it be a worthwhile goal to write at least one letter of appreciation each and every week. If you choose to make this a goal you will be touching at least 52 people per year in a very special way.

10. Hugs

It has been researched and found a person needs four hugs per day to just survive, eight hugs per day to maintain and twelve hugs per day to grow.

The Surgeon General has determined hugging is good for your health. Hugging is practically perfect: No movable parts, no batteries to wear out, no periodic check-ups, low energy consumption, high energy yield, inflation-proof, non-fattening, no monthly payments, no insurance requirements, theft-proof, non-taxable, non-polluting, and, of course, fully returnable. Hugging is all natural: Organic, naturally sweet, no pesticides, no preservatives, no artificial ingredients, and 100% wholesome. The best people, places and times to hug: Anyone, anywhere and anytime.

If you want more information on hugs, read "The Hug Therapy Book" by Kathleen Keating. It is humorous and enjoyable reading that makes the point that we all need hugs.

Poem

The Touch Of The Master's Hand

Myra Brooks Welch

'Twas battered and scared, and the auctioneer
   Thought it scarcely worth his while
To waste much time on the old violin,
   But he held it up with a smile.

"What am I bidden, good folks", he cried.
   "Who'll start the bidding for me"?
"A dollar, a dollar", then "two. Only two?
   Two dollars, and who'll make it three"?

"Three dollars, once; three dollars, twice;
   Going for three ...." but no,
From the room far back, a grey haired man
   Came forward and picked up the bow;

Then wiping the dust from the old violin,
   He tighten the loose strings,
He played a melody pure and sweet
   As a caroling angel sings.

The music ceased, and the auctioneer,
   With a voice that was quite a low,

Said "What am I bid for the old violin"?
  As he held it up with the bow.

"A thousand dollars, and who'll make it two?
  Two thousand, and who'll make it three?
Three thousand, once; three thousand, twice;
  And going, and gone", said he.

The people cheered, but some of them cried,
  "We do not quite understand,
What changed it's worth"? Swiftly came the reply:
  "The touch of a master's hand".

And many a man with life out of tune,
  And battered and scarred with sin,
Is auctioned cheap to the thoughtless crowd,
  Much like the old violin.

A "mess of pottage", a glass of wine;
  A game and he travels on.
He's "going" once; and "going" twice;
  He's "going and almost gone".

But the master comes, and the foolish crowd
  Never can quite understand.
The worth of a soul and the change that's wrought
  By the touch of the Master's hand.

Enthusiasm

The fourth step in *The C.A.R.E Principles* is building lasting enthusiasm. The key to pulling everything together is to develop unlimited enthusiasm. Enthusiasm is the element that inspires us to greater achievement and success. You can sell your ideas, your products, your services or yourself to others if you approach them enthusiastically. The word "enthusiasm" means "God within". With enthusiasm you can move the mountains of doubt and negative thinking from your life for good.

Norman Vincent Peale said, "*You can put new spirit, new creative skill into your job. Indeed, you can do better with everything. Enthusiastic, zest-packed living is yours if you want it. I have seen the tremendous things enthusiasm has done for so many. Believe me, it works"!*

B. C. Forbes, of Forbes Magazine, said, *"Enthusiasm is the all-essential human jet propeller. It is the driving force which elevates men to miracle workers. It begets boldness, courage, kindles confidence, and overcomes doubts. It creates endless energy, the source of all accomplishment".*

Frank Betcher in his book, How I Raised Myself From Failure To Success In Selling, talks about the time he was playing baseball and was moved from the major league to the minors because he played "deadpan" ball. On a hot summer day he decided he would play with enthusiasm and he did. He was noticed and within a short period of time was moved back to the majors with a large increase in pay. **He found if you "act" enthusiastic you will become enthusiastic.** It was a lesson he never forgot and it served him well through his careers in both baseball and selling.

Enthusiasm is the second most contagious thing in the world today. Do you know what is the first most contagious thing in the world today?

"Lack of Enthusiasm"

Most people find it is very easy to be enthusiastic when everything is coming up roses. It is when you have one of those days, when you only open your mouth to change feet, it is difficult to remember you are an enthusiastic person.

Lack of enthusiasm on your part or those around you can affect how everything goes during the day. Have you ever been really enthusiastic in the morning, but when you got to the office someone was sick, another got a ticket coming to work, another just ached all over? How did your enthusiasm hold up? What do you do when you're surrounded by unenthusiastic people?

You need a trigger that will break through the negativism and allow the enthusiasm inside to continue to flow out.

The C.A.N.

One thing you can do is use "The C.A.N." (Comments Are Negative) at the coffee pot where you work. The "The C.A.N." works this way: You take a three pound coffee can and decorate it so it is bright and shiny. Then place it near the coffee pot in the morning. Anyone can say anything they want, as long as it is positive. If anyone says anything negative, it costs them a dollar which they must put in "The C.A.N.". At the end of the first month you take everyone out to dinner on the money in "The C.A.N. The second month you probably will only have enough money to buy donuts. After the third month, you most likely will no longer need "The C.A.N.". By the way, if anyone says two negative things its two dollars even if they say them in the same sentence. For example, "It is an ugly day outside and I don't feel good either" would be two dollars in 'The C.A.N.".

Ball of Fire

Years ago, when I was teaching Dale Carnegie Courses, we would work on teaching people to be ten times more enthusiastic than they presently were. One of the most positive techniques I found to help people get enthusiastic and stay enthusiastic was to have them leap out of bed in the morning and when their feet hit the floor, shout "*I'm a ball of fire*"! This would give them the positive start in the morning and get them going for the day.

Red Dots

The problem people had was they were enthusiastic to start, but it was difficult to stay enthusiastic through the day. To keep enthusiasm running through the day I found the best trigger is putting a red dot on your watch. The average person looks at their watch a minimum of 30 times per day and as much as 300 times per day. When you look at your watch the red dot will trigger your subconscious memories of enthusiasm and will break through the negative atmosphere.

Use a red dot on your watch because it will remind you:

I Am A Ball Of Fire!!!

If you don't wear a watch, put the red dot on your cell phone or somewhere where you will see it throughout the day.

A sure way of maintaining your enthusiasm is to associate with enthusiastic people. All of us need a support group of one sort or another. You should have a support group of enthusiastic people.

Make a list of the enthusiastic people you know.

1. _____

2. _____

3. _____

4. _____

5. _____

6. _____

7. _____

8. _____

9. _____

10. _____

While you have these people in mind, think of the personality traits they exhibit. Make a list of ten of the traits enthusiastic people exhibit.

1. _____

2. _____

3. _____

4. _____

5. _____

6. _____

7. _____

8. _____

9. _____

10. _____

How many of the top ten personality traits do you personally have? Remember if you act out the trait you will acquire the trait. Now list the five traits you will set your goals to acquire over the next 21 days.

1. _____

2. _____

3. _____

4. _____

5. _____

What are you willing to do to improve your enthusiasm and acquire the traits you listed?

_____

_____

_____

_____

_____

_____

_____

_____

Count Your Blessings

What do you believe in? List at least six things you believe in:

_____

_____

_____

_____

_____

_____

_____

_____

_____

_____

_____

_____

_____

_____

_____

_____

_____

O. B. A. Cards

Using an O. B. A. Card will keep your enthusiasm peeked and will be the trigger to a positive goal achieving life. O. B. A. stands for Objective, Blessings and Achievements. Fill in the O. B. A. sheet below and then transfer the information to a 3 X 5 card to carry with you at all times.

Objective:

_____

_____

_____

_____

Blessings:

_____

_____

_____

_____

John C Erdman

Achievements:

_____

_____

_____

_____

_____

Poems

You Are

As young as your faith;
As old as your doubts;
As young as your self-confidence;
As old as your fears;
As young as your hope;
As old as your despair.

Years may wrinkle the skin, but
to give up enthusiasm wrinkles
the soul.
Anonymous

The Optimist's Creed

Promise yourself:

To be so strong nothing can disturb your peace of mind.

To talk health, happiness and prosperity to every person you meet.

To make all your friends feel that there is something in them.

To look at the sunny side of everything and make your optimism come true.

To think only of the best, work only for the best and expect only the best.

To be just as enthusiastic about the success of others as you are about your own.

To forget the mistakes of the past and press on to the greater achievements of the future.

To wear a cheerful countenance at all times and give every living creature you meet a smile.

To give so much time to the improvement of yourself that you have no time to criticize others.

To be too large for worry, too noble for anger, too strong for fear, and too happy to permit the presence of trouble.

Optimists International

Summary of The C.A.R.E Principles

Commitment

1. Move your desires into goals by getting them into the physical realm.
2. Assess the "As Is" situation and write it down.
3. Establish the "Target Point" and write it down.
4. Select the goals, set the time tables and put them in writing.
5. Determine there are no conflicts.
6. Commit yourself by knowing the "Whys".
7. Start working on the "Bite-Size" pieces.
8. Follow up and change as necessary.

Attitudes

1. Realize we play "Old Memories" and they cause us to sometimes act in the negative mode.
2. Use positive self-talk.
3. Do a "profit and loss" statement on yourself at least once per quarter.
4. Write affirmations that change negative memories to positive memories and repeat them out loud twice per day.
5. Use quick affirmations throughout your day and especially after you make the "Delete, Delete" statement.
6. Recognize your success patterns.
7. Use positive imaging.

Relationships

1. Remember the three personalities we are dealing with in each contact with other people.
2. Remember the four ways in which we judge and are judged by other people.
3. Earning Your Way Through Trust.
4. Use the Nine Human Relation concepts.
5. It is healthy and OK to hug other people.

Enthusiasm

1. Act enthusiastic and you will become enthusiastic.
2. Use a "The C.A.N." around the coffee pot at work.
3. Use a red dot to remind yourself that you're a "Ball Of Fire"!
4. Associate with enthusiastic people.
5. Assume the traits of enthusiastic people.
6. Become an "Optimist".

John C Erdman

About The Author

John C. Erdman
"Mr. Enthusiasm"

After a review of Mr. Erdman's career it will become apparent why he enjoys the prestige of being listed in several "Who's Who" directories, including "Who's Who in Training and Development in America."

With an academic background in advertising art, photography, business management and psychology, he launched his business career in the training industry. He has been responsible for creating and implementing extensive training programs in sales, customer relations, management techniques and personal development.

Mr. Erdman is also a former, fully certified instructor for all five of the Dale Carnegie Courses and taught them in several key locations across the United States, including introducing and instructing the courses in several parts of Alaska.

For over twenty years, he has helped thousands of career minded people reach their goals for success through instruction on enthusiasm, effective speaking, human relations, sales techniques, customer relation concepts, personal development, management methods and self- image psychology.

Over the years, thousands of people have also been motivated toward self-improvement and success by hearing Mr. Erdman's high performance speeches before many groups, organizations and conventions. Several of these speeches are: "Don't Kill My Cat", "Beyond Here Be Dragons", "Turn Your Stumbling Blocks Into Stepping Stones", "Be An A.C.E." and "Become A Ball Of Fire".

Mr. Erdman's professional improvement and success workshops include: The C.A.R.E. Principles (a personal and leadership development course and book); Professional Selling Workshop (a professional selling skills course); Effective Presentations Workshop (a public speaking skills course); Professional Customer Service Workshop (a customer service course); Effective Time Management

Workshop (a time and personal management course). All these programs not only teach the techniques and skills involved, but also develop the confidence to use them.

You can reach John at:

Website - www.ideal-companies.com

Blog - www.jcerdman.com

Email – john@ideal-companies.com

DATE DUE

AUG - - 2015

23457680R00081

Made in the USA
Middletown, DE
25 August 2015